Shark
ALLEY

Rob Waring, *Series Editor*

HEINLE
CENGAGE Learning™

Australia • Brazil • Japan • Korea • Mexico • Singapore • Spain • United Kingdom • United States

Words to Know

This story is set in South Africa. It takes place near the coast of the Cape of Good Hope in the village of Gansbaai [gænsbɑɪ] and around Dyer Island.

A **Sharks!** Read the definitions. Then complete the paragraph with the correct forms of the words or phrases.

bait: food used to catch animals and fish
cage diving: going into the ocean in a cage to observe sea life safely
extinct: no longer in existence
predator: an animal that lives by killing and eating other animals
shark: a large, typically meat-eating fish which can be dangerous

'Shark Alley' is a narrow waterway near South Africa where a large number of great white (1)_____ gather. These huge fish may one day become (2)_____, so many people want to see them before it's too late. To do this, diving boat operators take people on boats to go (3)_____, so they can see sharks in their natural environment. Boat operators often put (4)_____ or blood in the water to attract sharks to the dive sites. Since the shark is the largest (5)_____ in the fish family, many people are concerned that this association between food and people is a dangerous one.

Cage Diving with a Great White Shark

shark

B **Shark Research.** Read the paragraph. Then match each word with the correct definition.

There is currently a controversy about whether or not cage diving causes sharks to attack humans. Biologists are doing research to determine if sharks are more aggressive when people are cage diving nearby. Near Dyer Island, the natural prey of the great white shark are seabirds, like penguins, or sea animals, such as seals. Therefore, researchers are putting decoys that look like these animals into the water and observing how the sharks attack them when cage divers are near.

1. controversy _____
2. aggressive _____
3. prey _____
4. penguin _____
5. seal _____
6. decoy _____

a. an animal with smooth, dark fur that eats fish and lives near the sea
b. something used to trick someone or something into an action
c. a large, flightless, black-and-white seabird
d. behaving in a violent way
e. animals killed for food by other animals
f. a public disagreement, usually involving strong opinions about an important subject

cage

Welcome to 'Shark Alley,' one of the few places in the world where great white sharks **roam**.[1] Every year, large numbers of tourists visit this narrow waterway off the coast of South Africa to see the great white sharks that often gather in the area. Local dive boat operators here take tourists cage diving so that they can see sharks in their natural underwater environment. In order to ensure that their customers get to see sharks in action, the operators often bait the sharks with fish parts and blood. Some think that by doing this, they make these huge monsters of the deep more active so they may come close enough for the divers to touch—if they dare.

However, these days the great white sharks, or 'great whites' as they are sometimes called, are part of a large controversy. People are wondering if cage diving might be turning the world's largest predatory fish into a hunter of humans. Recently, an increasing incidence of shark attacks on people has caused local surfers and swimmers to become extremely worried. One young woman, a surfer, talks about the alarming rise in attacks. "There's just started to be more and more attacks," she says, "more friends of ours, people that we actually knew." Is baiting the sharks **conditioning**[2] these creatures to think of humans as food? Two men want to find out: biologist Brady Barr, and shark researcher Ryan Johnson.

---

[1]**roam:** move freely over a large area
[2]**condition:** shape the attitudes or behavior of someone or something

CD 1, Track 07

Fact or Opinion?

Look at the following statements. Write 'F' for those that are factual, or 'O' for those that are an opinion.

1. Every year large numbers of tourists visit South Africa to go cage diving, _____.

2. Using bait makes sharks more active. _____

3. Sharks are part of a great controversy. _____

4. Cage diving is turning sharks into eaters of humans. _____

In order to find out whether the sharks are perceiving human beings as food, Brady Barr needs to learn more about these huge animals. As part of his research, he plans to take advantage of the opportunity to swim with the great white sharks. To initiate his plans, he's going directly to the source of the controversy: Shark Alley. Shark Alley is located near the town of Gansbaai, which is on the tip of South Africa's Cape of Good Hope, or the 'Cape.'

Gansbaai has long been known as the great white shark capital of the world and is considered to be the place to go if one wants to see these amazing animals. Dyer Island is located just off the coast of the Cape near Gansbaai, and just off Dyer Island is a place called 'Geyser Rock,' which is home to thousands of cape fur seals. The water is thick with seals, which attract large numbers of sharks due to the fact that seals are a primary food source for them. Great whites often swim up and down the **channel**[3] hunting the seals, which has earned this section of the ocean the name 'Shark Alley.'

---

[3] **channel:** narrow waterway

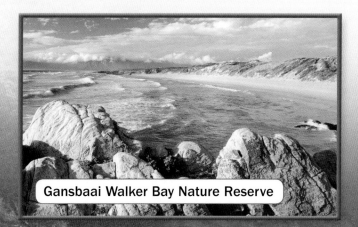

Gansbaai Walker Bay Nature Reserve

An entire tourist industry has developed in this area of South Africa which is based on people who come to dive with the sharks. There's no doubt that many tourists are attracted to the idea of swimming with deadly sharks— as long as they can remain safely protected behind the walls of a cage. The controversy develops when the dive operators throw bait into the water to obtain more shark activity for their customers. The questions then become: What actually happens if you use bait to attract sharks to humans? Do the sharks learn to think of people as food? The answers to these questions could potentially ruin an entire tourist economy.

In order to get to the bottom of the problem, someone needs to answer the basic question: Is the trend towards cage diving turning the great whites into eaters of humans? Luckily, Ryan Johnson and Brady Barr are ready to find out. Ryan Johnson is a shark researcher from New Zealand who works at his computer as well as at sea to find out more about sharks. Ryan explains what he does when it comes to sharks. "My research really **entails**[4] looking at the predatory behavior of the white shark," he says. However, this time, biologist Brady Barr is going to accompany Ryan on a visit to Shark Alley. Together, the two hope to reveal more about shark behavior and the possible dangers of cage diving for swimmers and surfers.

_____

[4]**entail:** consist of; include

Scan for Information

Scan page 11 to answer these questions.

1. What time of day do Ryan and Brady go to Shark Alley?

2. What do they plan to do there?

3. What do they use to attract sharks?

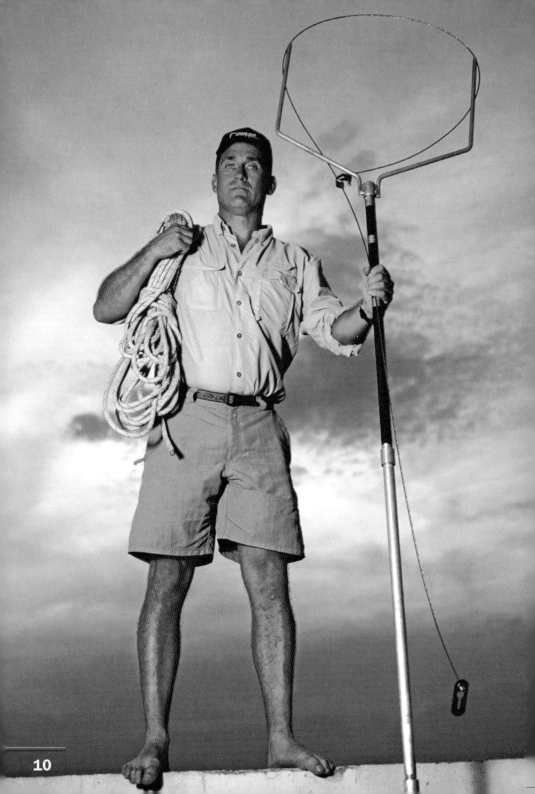

It's very early in the morning when Ryan and Brady guide their small boat out to sea. As they slow their boat in the Shark Alley area, the sun is only beginning to rise in the sky. The pair of researchers wants to arrive at the shark 'hot spot' before anyone else does. Ryan plans to **monitor**[5] the sharks' behavior before the cage-dive operators arrive. Then he'll be able to observe whether or not the arrival of the boats affects how aggressive the sharks are.

First, Ryan uses decoys to draw the sharks near to the boat so he can measure their aggressiveness when they attack. As he throws the decoys, which look like the sharks' usual prey of seals and penguins, in the water, Ryan describes them. "These are designed to sort of **resemble**[6] the natural prey, the larger prey of the shark," he says. Ryan and Brady throw more decoys into the water and attach ropes to connect them to the boat. Once the decoys are set, all that the two researchers need to do is wait for the first attack; but they have no idea when—or if— it will come.

---

[5]**monitor:** watch; observe the actions of someone or something
[6]**resemble:** look like something or someone else

A Seal Decoy

Suddenly, after a short wait, a shark appears, and the two men start shouting with excitement. "There it is! Oh my gosh! Look at that thing!" says Brady Barr as an **enormous**[7] great white swims near the decoy. There's no doubt that seeing a great white shark close up is a remarkable experience. "What's he doing, what's he doing?" asks the biologist as the shark swims past the decoy. "Oh, man, he's huge! Look at him!" continues Barr, thrilled to see the great white. The two men watch as the shark cautiously circles its prey.

As the shark nears the boat, the two men notice its appearance, and try to predict its next move. "He's going to go for it! Is that him?" says Brady. Once they are sure that it is the same shark and that it is interested in food, Brady begs the shark to just take a bite of the decoy, "Come on, baby! Hit it!" he says. Unfortunately, the shark swims past the decoy once again without so much as a bite. But then, luckily, the big fish turns and approaches the decoy once more. "Here he comes. Here he comes," shout the two men together, followed by a victorious "He's got it!" when the shark finally takes the decoy in its huge mouth. The two researchers look on as the shark attempts to bite through the decoy as it would with its normal food. As the shark turns and rolls and tries to tear its prey apart, the researchers carefully observe its level of aggression.

―――――――――――――

[7]**enormous:** very big; huge

Later, more sharks appear and the team has a chance to observe several attacks on their decoys. As they do, Ryan rates each shark for aggressiveness by giving it a score from one to five. In the most aggressive attack, a huge shark hits the decoy with such force that part of the shark's body leaves the water. Barr can do nothing but say, "Look at the size of that thing! Look at him!" as the shark locks his knife-sharp teeth onto the decoy and shakes its head violently as it tries to eat it. This particular shark receives a rating of five out of five for aggression. After the shark leaves, Ryan recovers the decoy, but when it comes out of the water, he can see that it definitely needs repairing. The shark has almost bitten the solidly built decoy in two!

As the day continues, the cage-dive operators begin to appear in Shark Alley and start baiting the sharks to encourage them to approach the cages. The question on the two researchers' minds remains: Will the bait cause the sharks to become more aggressive, just as the surfers fear? Ryan and Brady must wait to find out. It generally takes a little time for the sharks to react to the arrival of the boats. So, while Ryan monitors the sharks' behavior, Brady decides to visit a cave-diving boat. He wants to see just how the cage-dive operators interact with the animals.

Ryan gives Brady a ride to a nearby diving boat and then speeds back to the research site to continue monitoring the aggression of the sharks. The cage-dive operators quickly prepare for Brady's dive by dropping a huge cage over the side of the boat and starting to put bait in the water. It's not long before a big shark begins to follow the bait. Now it's Brady's chance to see what cage diving is really like. He quickly puts on his **wetsuit**[8] and other diving equipment and prepares to enter the water. When he notices the enormous shark circling near him in the sea, he comments: "Man, that is huge! I want to get in the cage!"

Finally, Brady has everything he needs and carefully steps down into the cage. Getting into and out of the safety cage is the most dangerous time for the diver. If he or she makes one wrong move or slips, the diver could end up in the water with the shark. If that happens, the person could easily be attacked, injured, or even killed. Luckily, Brady manages to get into the cage without any problems and is lowered down into the deep, **murky**[9] water.

Once he's safely underwater inside the cage, Barr looks anxiously around; he can't see the shark at all because the water is so unclear. He has no idea from which direction the great white will come, so he must wait with his camera and hope for a chance to take photographs. Finally, the shark swims out of the murky depths and advances slowly towards the cage, but then disappears again into the darkness. Brady loses sight of the large predator completely, but then suddenly...

[8]**wetsuit:** a special suit made of rubber worn when diving
[9]**murky:** dirty; unclear

The whole cage rocks in the water as the huge shark approaches the cage and shakes the entire structure! The shark is trying to get its **massive**[10] head between the safety bars of the cage to get Brady. Barr quickly throws himself down low in the cage to get back from the huge teeth of the fish. Then suddenly, it's over just as quickly as it began and the monster fish swims off into the deep.

Nevertheless, it's an extremely frightening moment, and Barr decides to surface so he can breathe some fresh air. As his head and shoulders emerge from the water at the top of the cage, he pauses before turning around to signal that he wants a break. But then he hears someone shout "Brady!" As he looks around confusedly, he realizes that the man in the diving boat is shouting in an alarmed voice, "Go down! Go down! Go down!" The shark has silently reappeared, and it's far too dangerous for Barr to leave the cage at this time. Just as he lowers himself back into the water, the shark hits the cage again—hard. All Brady can see are the dangerous fish's enormous teeth on the outside of the cage. Brady is trapped!

---

[10]**massive:** very large in size

Finally, after a few anxious moments, the shark swims away, and Barr can make his escape at last. He surfaces and the boat operators pull him out of the water quickly, shouting, "Go! Go! Go!" to encourage him to move faster. The last thing they need now is for the shark to come back for another visit. It could hit the cage again and get a chance to attack. As he comes out of the water, Brady is shouting and very excited about what he has experienced below. Everyone else is simply glad to have him safely back in the boat.

While all of the excitement is taking place on the diving boat, Ryan is still working hard back on the research boat. He's finishing up his study on cage diving and its impact on the sharks. As a result of his research, Ryan has found that the boats do have a temporary, or short-term, effect on the sharks' behavior, but the impact is the opposite of what one might expect.

Ryan takes a moment to discuss the results of his studies. He explains that, in his opinion, there is a difference between the short-term and longer-term effects of cage diving on the sharks. "I think it's becoming clear that there is a short-term impact on their behavior, an immediate impact," he says. "When the shark operators are there with their bait in the water and the shark has an opportunity to come up there and [put his] mouth [on] this bait," he explains, "it does seem to put them more in a **scavenging mode of mind**."[11]

However, Ryan has found further information that is the opposite of what was expected. His initial discovery about short-term effects is part of an even more interesting find. He argues that the sharks' active hunting **instincts**[12] may actually be switched off during cage diving. He feels that this is because the fish are constantly exposed to dead bait. His theory is that this actually makes them less aggressive, rather than more aggressive. Ryan has also noted that the sharks tend to go back to their normal, more aggressive behavior once the boats leave.

---

[11]**scavenging mode of mind:** *(unusual use)* in the mood to search for food
[12]**instinct:** a natural, unlearned behavior or ability

Ryan has also developed some theories regarding the long-term effects of cage diving on the shark population. From his observations, Johnson is confident that the cage divers are not training the sharks to eat people. The main reason for his conclusion is that the sharks do not have enough time in contact with the divers to become conditioned. The basis for this theory seems to be that the sharks of 'Shark Alley' are usually in transit. He explains, "I'm working with the sharks every day, and truthfully, they don't stay in this area long. Maybe one day, two max[imum]."

According to Ryan, one or two days of **exposure**[13] to an activity is simply not long enough to train these massive fish to do something. He explains: "No animal can be conditioned when you've only got that one day of interaction. I can't imagine how that can be conditioning in that sense." So, according to Ryan, the shark tourism trend does not lead to more shark attacks, but how does Brady feel after his exciting experience?

---

[13]**exposure:** experiencing or being affected by something in a specific situation or area

Both as a biologist and active conservationist, Barr is thrilled by what he's seen and experienced in Shark Alley. During his time on the water, Brady also noticed that the tourists on the diving boats were quite impressed and often came back with a greater **appreciation**[14] for these amazing creatures. He reports: "Everybody I saw that went out on one of those boats stepped off the boat back on the dock and they were just like, 'Wow, that was one of the most amazing things I've ever done! Those are incredible animals!'" In theory, this kind of increased respect could be a huge help in saving an animal that may one day become extinct due to overfishing and other factors.

The tourists are not the only ones who have developed an appreciation for these incredible animals. After diving with the sharks, Brady feels extremely thankful for the chance to have seen a great white, up close. "A day doesn't go by where I don't think about my experiences with those animals," he explains. "I mean, it's amazing. No matter where I'm at or what I'm doing, at some point, I **find my mind drifting**[15] back to seeing those great white sharks." Apparently, for many people, a visit to Shark Alley is an unforgettable experience and the chance of a lifetime.

---

[14]**appreciation:** a high regard for the beauty or complexity of something

[15]**find (one's) mind drifting:** discover that one's thoughts are going in unexpected or unplanned directions

Summarize

Decide whether you are for or against cage diving and write a persuasive report about the topic. Support your opinion with facts and information from this book or other sources.

After You Read

1. What is the main purpose of page 4?
   A. to describe a great white shark
   B. to explain the controversy about cage diving
   C. to introduce some boat operators
   D. to give instructions on how to bait a shark

2. Which word on page 7 can be replaced by 'get started with'?
   A. find out
   B. initiate
   C. attract
   D. earned

3. Some people believe sharks are attacking humans because:
   A. The sharks are protecting themselves.
   B. The tourists are disturbing the sharks.
   C. The sharks are confusing humans with seals.
   D. The bait is attracting sharks to humans.

4. What is something the scientists do NOT use to measure the sharks aggressiveness?
   A. a boat
   B. prey
   C. a rope
   D. a decoy

5. Which is a suitable heading for paragraph 2 on page 12?
   A. Baby Shark Takes Bite
   B. Scientists Fearful of Great White
   C. Giant Shark Fooled by Decoy
   D. Shark Bites Researchers

6. Why does Brady Barr say that he wants to get in the cage on page 16?
   A. because he is scared of the shark
   B. because his equipment is not operating correctly
   C. because he needs to get back to Johnson quickly
   D. because he wants to start his research

7. Brady Barr is anxious _____ he can't see.
   A. while
   B. when
   C. who
   D. where

8. How did Barr probably feel during the event in the cage described on page 19?
   A. disgusted
   B. abandoned
   C. deserving
   D. exposed

9. What does the word 'impact' mean in paragraph 2 on page 20?
   A. evidence
   B. effect
   C. benefit
   D. hypothesis

10. What conclusion does Ryan Johnson reach on page 23?
   A. The bait has no effect on the sharks.
   B. The effect of the bait on sharks is unclear.
   C. The bait makes the sharks less aggressive.
   D. The bait makes the sharks more aggressive.

11. According to Johnson, what is required to condition a white shark?
   A. Different experiences in different locations.
   B. The same experiences for one day.
   C. Different experiences in the same location.
   D. The same experiences over a long period of time.

12. What does Barr think is an important benefit of cage diving?
   A. It teaches people to value great white sharks.
   B. It encourages people to come to South Africa.
   C. It gives people a memory they will never forget.
   D. All of the above.

http://www.shark+central.org

Welcome to
SHARK CENTRAL!

Shark Central is a website committed to reducing the world's fear of sharks.

DANGEROUS SHARKS: WHERE ARE THEY?

Sharks can be found almost everywhere including northern Europe, East Asia, and South America. Of the total number of types of sharks in the world, very few are actually associated with human injury. The coastal areas in Australia host a diverse number of sharks, to which several attacks on humans per year are attributed. However, these attacks average only a single death per year. The east and west coasts of the United States also report between 20 and 40 shark attacks each year. However, these areas have thousands of miles of beaches and a very large population of people who use them during their free time. We have invaded the sharks' domain, and they may not know how to deal with this.

Comparison of Five Types of Sharks			
Name	Size	Life Expectancy	Dangerous to Humans?
Basking Shark	6-8 meters	73 years	No
Tiger Shark	4-6 meters	Unknown	Yes
Great White Shark	4-5 meters	30-40 years	Yes
Nurse Shark	up to 3.5 meters	Unknown	Rarely
Long-Nose Saw Shark	about 1 meter	10-15 years	No

Imagine That!

- Sharks never run out of teeth: if one is lost, another tooth moves forward from the rows of reserve teeth.

- Sometimes sharks eat other sharks, however not all sharks eat meat.

- One big meal can last a shark for over three months.

- Two-thirds of a shark's brain is linked to its sense of smell.

WHY DO SHARKS ATTACK HUMANS?

The truth is that incidences of shark attacks are actually very rare. In fact, humans kill more sharks each year than sharks kill people. Considering the millions of sharks and millions of people in the world's oceans, the 71 proven attacks on humans in 2008 seems to be an extremely small number. Although the number of shark attacks is rising slightly each year, researchers attribute this to the human population growth. They feel it is a result of the fact that more people are spending time in the water—not an increasingly dangerous shark population. Almost all studies show that shark attacks are the exception, not the rule.

WHY DON'T SHARKS LEAVE US ALONE?

When a shark attacks a human, it is not a calculated choice. It's usually a mistake. When they see hands moving and feet kicking, it looks like either a threat to their safety, or a wounded animal which would make an easy meal. Sometimes in murky water, a shark may mistake a human for a penguin, seal or other natural prey. The fact that they almost always swim away immediately after biting seems to indicate that sharks do not purposely pursue and attack humans.

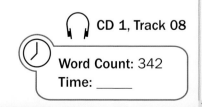

CD 1, Track 08

Word Count: 342
Time: _____

Vocabulary List

aggressive (3, 11, 12, 15, 16, 23)
appreciation (26)
bait (2, 4, 5, 8, 15, 16, 23)
cage dive (2, 3, 4, 5, 8, 11, 15, 16, 20, 23, 24, 27)
channel (7)
condition (4, 24)
controversy (3, 4, 5, 7, 8)
decoy (3, 11, 12, 15)
enormous (12, 16, 19)
entail (8)
exposure (24)
extinct (2, 26)
find (one's) mind drifting (26)
instinct (23)
massive (19, 24)
monitor (11, 15, 16)
murky (16)
penguin (3, 11,)
predator (2, 4, 8, 16)
prey (3, 11, 12)
resemble (11)
roam (4)
scavenging mode of mind (23)
seal (3, 7, 11)
shark (2, 3, 4, 5, 7, 8, 9, 11, 12, 15, 16, 19, 20, 23, 24, 26)
wetsuit (16)